The Picnic Tree

Story by Jacquie Kilkenny
Photography by Lindsay Edwards

Jade and Mia
loved playing at Treetop Park.

Today, they were going
to have a picnic lunch there.

Jade helped Mum with the basket
and Mia took the rug.

"Let's have our lunch here,
by this big tree," said Jade.
"This looks like a good place."

The girls put the rug down on the grass.

A cold wind started to blow.

"Quick!" shouted Jade. "The rug's flying away."

"We will have to tie it down,"
laughed Jade.

"I'm sorry, Jade," said Mum.
"It's too cold and windy
to have a picnic today.
We will come back tomorrow."

"Where's Mia?" said Mum.

"Mia! Mia!" shouted Jade.
"We are going home, now."

Jade turned around,
and then she saw her.

Mia was hiding under the big tree.
The branches went right down
to the ground.

Jade pushed some of the branches
out of the way,
and climbed under the tree, too.

"Mia, we have to go home,"
said Jade.
"It's too windy for a picnic today."

"It's not windy under here,"
laughed Mia.
"And there is lots of room
to have a picnic."

"This **is** a good place," laughed Jade.

"We will call this our picnic tree."